Some Gangster Pain

Some Gangster Pain

Poems by
Gillian Conoley

Carnegie Mellon University Press
Pittsburgh 1987

Acknowledgements

Grateful acknowledgement is made to the editors of the following
magazines, where some of these poems first appeared:

American Poetry Review: "Correctional House," "Murder in a Small Town."
Confrontation: "July 5, 1985."
Cricket: "Goat Without Horns."
Hubbub: "Letter, 1945."
Intro 12: "The Invention of Texas."
Ironwood: "Mad Snow."
The North American Review: "Premature Reincarnation."
Ploughshares: "Alias," "Some Gangster Pain," "Suddenly the Graves."
Tendril: "The Mexico Divorce Hotel," "The Sound I Make Leaving,"
    "Tonight I Feel Mortal," "Patsy Cline," "Woman Speaking Inside Film
    Noir," "The Cousin at the Funeral," "New in Town," "The Tooth
    Fairy," "Insomnia."
Three Rivers Poetry Journal: "The Sky Fills Everything," "After the
    Baptism."
Yankee: "The Winter Babies."

Some of these poems also appeared in a limited edition chapbook,
Woman Speaking Inside Film Noir, (Lynx House Press, 1984).

I would also like to thank The MacDowell Colony.

Publication of this book is supported by grants from the National
    Endowment for the Arts in Washington, D.C., a Federal agency, and
    from the Pennsylvania Council on the Arts.

Carnegie Mellon University Press books are distributed by
    Harper and Row, Publishers.

Library of Congress Catalog Number 86-70209
ISBN 0-88748-026-8
ISBN 0-88748-027-6 Pbk.

Contents

Part I

Part II

Part III

For Domenic

Where bullets fly on the wind,
I am left in envy of the cowboys,
left admiring even the horses.

—Pablo Neruda

. . . the glory of his nostrils is
terrible.

Job 39:20

Part I

The Invention of Texas

The sea left this place
to fend for its own water,
leaving prickly wind
and one yellow color.

Birth continued.
Coyotes sang to cyclones on the lope,
men chattered in caves
in a kind of scat orchestration.

Someone invented the wheel.
This begat a misunderstanding
of circles. The Indians looked askance and blew
hollow smoke. Mexicans slept in

circumferences of corn
(in fact were the first to see corn as curio).
Soon they began to stay up all night
watching the stalks,
mistrusting the green dance.

The white man,
whose spherical countenance
was at first viewed as incomplete moon,
beat everyone up,
lassoed the stars and rode amuck,
spilling trails of sequins.

Patsy Cline

When I'm alone, I like how my nylons
mesh, the rustle I get
just walking.

I keep walking this way,
moving down the stage
like it was ice. Not like she did
in that yellow skirt,
strolling in
so everyone saw. You keep telling

the story a different way,
how nothing matters
outside this room. The thin coins
dropping out your pants.

But I still see
that bar, the lights
strung bare above every man's back,
the sticky perfume,
her skirt a breeze you could carry.

Once I got home,
I draped sheets over the posts
so my bed was a chariot.
But you were cast in every crease,
thick and strange
as when you danced, your arms
swallowing her

like a hot jewel. Let me tell you
I was not born in the shack
you'd like to see me in
with a fork and lipsticked cigarettes.

I may be walking backwards onto this plane,
but you're looking
like some rat-eyed pimp,
some hillside jack on a slide.

Dare

In this town there is a long rope.
Discordant leaf-melodies
above a line of boys naked and lawless.

When they swing, they pass
their mother's good sons
walking drenched in holy water.

Each time the river sags
a little, invisibly,
winks to next in line.

The hemp flies back
wet and oily,
cold as their dripping fists.

Too often
they have felt lonely
without clothes,

but when they let go
they are like newborns
bending their blue knees,

their cry
not of the living
or dead, but the narrow between.

Murder in a Small Town

She must have thought God was in those trees.
No clues, just the open door
and curtains that billowed
as if birds, as if large birds
were caught in them. The sheriff said
it was broad daylight
he couldn't quit seeing, going back there
so many times, even at night
he could see her soul falling bit by bit
down the tall spears of moonlight, into his hands.

It got to where he couldn't go anywhere
without a prisoner in his face.
Behind a dining room window, someone spooned
white gravy onto a biscuit.
Someone pulled back a chair
meant to receive her body.
Who listened for the country western song
asleep on her lips?

The sheriff walked the night
to the end of town,
until he could see tractors
idle in fields,
and cattle start to feed. Until
he found his way through the grass
and lay his hands down,
hands he could no longer see in their natural size,
nothing above them anymore
but the flies, iridescent
and swarming frankly in the morning sun.

Rodeo

Maybe I was ten
in the graze land, chest-high
to the even out of her breath.
Her great head dipped
shy as doe, and I took the bit.
She was led, counter eights
around the barrels.

Strawberry roan,
and her life ain't been
no crystal stair,
the cowboy said
in his suit of light.
Sired by appaloosa.

Cattle cars jangled locks,
truckers honked
and she scared.
Reared, three quick bucks.
In her eyes
foals were flaming through hoops,
in the sudden whites
a noose fell
over the dark neck of a man and she

broke loose. I looked to the men
running through the gate.
Torrent of denim and red dust.
Go on, get her quick,
go on. And I took off
after her, my legs already bowed
from her body,
the spurs on my heels
dimming in the high grasses.

The Mexico Divorce Hotel

The two next door
have looked into each other's faces
long enough to know the story they want
to tell keeps ending,

that the brightly colored
airplanes are full of possible
friends. Off our wrought iron veranda,
seastacks jut in open notation, water
rears back divers

dropping from cliffs. In a repose
we are learning,
our faces tight as those caught
in a mirror when no one
looks, we point

at parrot fish in brochures,
the elk coral, shrug off
what he wants, what she
wants. We know we are another

event rounding the corner
with a sort of plume on it. We do
the streets, walk out
of the tableau of ourselves
at the wrong address, white rooms so final

we stick our smart necks
in two directions, loose on the luck
of the convertible's wind,
the light torched
between us, before us the glimpse

in the windshield,
the arrangement of what we have brought
with us, our hands under glass.

The Sound I Make Leaving

Always I am just returning in a blue dress,
tight and daring. You've come to see me
that way, tall and bringing
no objects. Through the anemic

twilight we drag
the weekend, wondering
if this town will stop or pull
its trigger. It's difficult:

looking for the linear
way to talk. I want to
stir the light of this room
from its slow fade, make our couch

a peninsula we could cling to,
let the window call
what won't come out of our mouths
until the neighbors
fall forward
from their porches
and the whole day is a question
we can't hear.

After the Baptism

Those of us who watched became ashamed
again. We rolled the programs in our hands,
walked the red carpet's cross
while altar boys pulled curtains.
At the reception,
men removed their jackets
in the heat, women's heels pocked
the lawn. The mother's eyes were parakeets
flickering proud to her girl's face,
then ours, then back.

Yellow ladders
curved up from the pool,
allowed a focal point
for the vacant stare of the teenager,
who, cross-legged in a lawn chair,
might have been underwater, my small talk
reaching her in the distorted sounds
of the preacher.

I wanted to ask: did you feel his hands
keeping you down while hosannas
shook water, three times,
through your white gown?
In the holy tank, did you sputter air
when your body swore,
with its own heaviness,
against this dying out of water?

The Cousin at the Funeral

Three in the afternoon,
                            my skirt
held up in one fist,
our grandmother not even cold, we waded
far down the river,
                    not stopping
until the tree moss
                    hung in sweeps
and there was shade. Even then
I thought of how
you would tell it:

                    years later, after making love
in a city,
            its noise clanging
below you, your lover
watching as you stare away from her
to speak. She strains

to see you then, the way
you must have looked,
                        tall in your suit,
and me, like you,
                    tanned and gangly
but a girl.

            You tell her
slowly, your voice carrying
                        until she begins to nod,
knowing the amber light,
the smell of the rotting trunks,
                        the glimpse of me, you,
lying there on the shore.

Slave Quarter

The French windows
have been left
ajar, curtained
with new lace shadowing
the zinc-white sink.
Not because the slave quarter
is turned apartment,
painted pink like crepe myrtle
or rotting watermelon,
but because Royal Street
needs a paint job,
the ghosts of slaves
have begun to move.
With their dignity,
their unfinished gestures.

With aprons
the women run
to catch black chips
falling off balconies
like an oily rain. Men stand
with their buckets, but the wind pours
from the rooftops,
tossing everything
out of reach.

It will be years
until the sun throws back
its sequined mask
and we party,
we carnival. Centuries

until the hound's voice
is silenced
in the taxi's horn.

They are going to lie down
next to us
as if nothing has happened.
And we are going to sit
a long time
with our vast wonder and fear,
looking down at them,
waiting for their carved faces
to let us in.

Part II

The Ancestors Speak

The shoes we left empty filled
With your talk of trouble
And the loud surf in your ear.

We are the great gang
Of marked men and women
Beautiful but bad. Dark-suited

And sanctified,
We are your fatted cells,
Your hot blood and bruise.

You are our modern zygote.
Our divisible egg upright
At the crossroads

Like a boy with an orchid.
If whatever ends with beginning
By ending begins, help our story

Take hold. We'll strut our whole selves
Inside you, stomp our sentence
In your mouth.

Bear us malice,
And you'll blacken the old tree.
The town's not the same.

We can't hold up
The one who falls.
Go willingly to the common deep.

The Winter Babies

The stars are moons
gone home. There is nothing
to do but sleep,
the bulb overhead dangling
like suet. They have

this life, a lumpy sack everyone
comes to admire. Mothers
watch the thin eyelids, faint blue
and glamorous. Insomniacs

climb stairs to see,
their hands twitching
the smallest gestures. There is nothing
but sleep. Inside them

perks a mob of mutes, the dark
dropping its thousand handkerchiefs.

Letter, 1945

It is hard to say
that I had wanted it.
My arms around the boxed shoulders of glory.

In the public hugs,
couples so beautiful
as they break away

and return, their hands
already envelopes held to the chest.
My friends' heels poke the corridor

of our home. In *Life* magazine,
the women of Okinawa
brush each other's hair

as on the Island of the Amazons,
in the season of men. Jars on my bureau
are stoppered

to age orchid and jasmine and gardenia,
but when my friends leave
I turn on the radio and let the smells

loose, invisible clouds of Okinawa.
Our Johnny he grows up good
under the strong chins of wheat.

He is looking more like you everyday,
although sometimes
he is just me

when I look at him in the fields,
the khaki color undulating
above his shoulders,

the way I get a premonition
of my own image
sitting in a photobooth,

though the lens is small
and there will be four versions,
with your jacket, and without.

Leah Callahan: 1882–1972

An oval-shaped photograph
in the hallway:
Leah in her flapper days,
coal black hair
curved to the side,
cigarettes, men
in the background. The town told
how a cotton baron from Atlantic City
married her, built
his mansion. Out back,
a cement pool, where she didn't care
that the farmers, plowing east,
could see
when she dropped her robe
and dove.

In August, when cotton burst
from the husk, she imagined a light snow
across the fields,
and herself a flower, the color
of fine, glistening porcelain,
floating over the pool's surface.

Always one of the farmers
called something
she couldn't make out,
though she was sure
the water stirred. And certainly
the cicadas, thick in the air,
meant a song, a scratched record
spinning above her.

Those afternoons
the future hovered
in the deepest fields she could see,

its heat rising in waves, then closer,
in the willow's matted hair.

Only when branches kept light
from the pool
would she go in
to the kitchen table, talc her body
sailor-white, wait
for the silhouette
at the screen door.

Zella's House

She had left everything exactly
as it was: her son's room,
white-sheeted and stale, roped off
since the war. Outside, the yard was blinding,
a greenhouse a few steps
away—elephant ears, clairvoyant,
mopping its windows
in what breeze there was.

And what did she call
the house, her fingers
breaking the soil for ferns.
Carved saloon, a cotton baron's
grand idea? Which room

did she think of once inside
the greenhouse—plants
exotic in a steamy bath—did she see
her beaded gowns hanging
in the closet, their elaborate suicides?

When her heart fluttered and emptied,
was it the powder room she saw—
double mirrors
tossing the light across her—
so that either way
she looked, her image: hair cornflower
blue, eyes wide with possibility,
cut into frames of locomotion,
multiple recognition: *it is I,*
me, echoing
through the glass,
cutting into the walls
as far as I can see.

Woman Speaking Inside Film Noir

What I want happens
not when the man leaning on a lamppost
stares up to my room and I meet his gaze
through the blinds, but in the moment after,
in the neon's pulse, when his cigarette
glows in the rain like a siren
and he looks away.

I go back to bed and imagine
the sound of his shoes
on the wooden stairs, flight
after flight; my pincurls loosening,
falling across the pillow
gentle as dropped bolts of bargain silk.

When the door flies open there's nothing
but the luminous band of the radio,
still he steps toward me
in a pyramid of light.
Our shadows yearn across the dresser,
my perfume bottles glisten
like shots of scotch. The mirror
is one more stilled moon
that wants the wish of him,
his face upturned,
astonished, cloudy as opal.

Scarlett, On All Hallows

The tea olive stills, the explored moon
rises. She's come back
older, more desperate.

Black dirt, tended, heaped
for one hundred years did not quiet
her skirts, every magnolia

tucking its brown edges
inward. The chameleon darts,
—green, black—

and the tangled garden curls
its noose. What is she
to do, white, female, the plantation

cut up somewhere in a will,
every time
she tries to speak

the soft cotton
blooming in her mouth.
Should she stand

in the garden, still as plaster,
take the lantern
from the painted boy?

By his side
she could
make peace.

His empty hand
curled in a loose fist,
polished feet

anchored in the dirt. And she
with the lantern,
her mouth

a torn hibiscus,
eyes so old and sorry
the light won't glow.

Her shadow forms, settles
past the arbor.
He is old stone.

She will be like him
until the night
swings free.

A Bad Girl's Book of Music

In the trees' maddening,
tarantella swirl,
there is a song that begins
you'll never know who she was,
and when I hum it,
all the parts of that night
gather: tight sweater,
peroxide hair, her spent luck
a lousy hand of suicide kings
and one-eyed jacks.

In the cemetary, when the trees
turned their backs to her,
when the boys' hands lied
through her body,
it was me who closed her heart
from each inanimate face.
When she dressed and walked off,
I stood outside her, and I watched
as her name tore
through the town like rain,
like a headless robber.

Again and again, I have returned
our sewn heart.
She has steadied the tarred sky,
the stars. When mesquite branches
wrestle the light
like a girl into a skirt,
I listen for her walk.

I have given her a forehead of flowers.
I have crossed and kept

her hands. And although no one sings,
I hear her,
although no one sings
I follow.

The Middle Name

for Curby

Flavia, some Latin
queen, a dark woman
with a fan.

This name that no one
says, but asks for, unlikely,
like a sister.

So we do not trust them.
We keep them secrets.
But our sisters
know. She'll tell
you this: the angels
orbit our beds
while we sleep, calling
the men we'll marry.

We push the nail's skin
so the moons show.
Off the line we tweeze
brassieres, huge white funnels,
wear them as hats.

Nights my sister waves
her paper fan,
and whispers
Flavia, Flavia,
until she thinks
I have fallen asleep,

but I lie thinking
of a swan
gliding undisturbed,
then a swan beating water and light
as it tears into air.

The Tooth Fairy

How easily they suppose me
a card queen,
thieving, but they are

only children. The others forget,
store these coins
until the faces fade. In nightgowns the mothers

tell my story, over and over,
how they have forgotten.
I do not come to their children

through a reticent fleet of veils,
the white breath of their hopeless curtains.
When the forest

took me away,
I took all my father's silver,
but there is no use for it

here. My gown
rummages in terrific foliage.
I know the children

don't want their rooms, that they are digging up
stones. The mothers rub
the green from every knee, and they sleep.

Each room contains a memory
I recognize: always there is
the surprise of myself in their mirrors,

how beautiful I have grown. I am sorry
for the knubby ivory
of their mouths,

but I must take something
to remember, and the children
are so drowsy, and grateful.

New in Town

Tonight a teenager
peels the foil from a gum wrapper, sees herself
floating. Her mother watches
television send its blue light
through the living room,
tell her what it is like
to live in Italy.
Outside white laundry waves goodbye.

This is not Italy.
In the glass-eyed window the manager stores
phials of dark mercury.
This town knows its pilgrims.

No one knows me,
though at the grocery there is a camera
rolling over my shoulder
as I select tangerines.
There are the tin moths stupidly hitting the light.

The fluorescent sidewalk,
which I can feel more easily than leaves,
bares its veins and I realize I
could be anyone.

Telephone numbers
drop from my pockets.
While the baker's not looking,
I change hats.

I carry a bouquet of oleanders
behind me, ready to flash.
I carry on.

Finally my feet ask the rest of me
is this the place? The I
I think I am
wants to answer
with the names that keep following me
from town to town,
or the sound I hear but cannot name,
maybe water, a foreign piano.

Drive In

In the last light full of dust and spheres
we would roll down the window
and hang the speaker, alien mouth
whose single utterance
was the muffled static of jabalina
on the roadside,
and as the show started
the light beamed across the car
so I saw its bones
like the bones of coyote surfacing
in a drought.

On the screen
there was more desert,
and men on horses riding through a darkness
black as a lake at night.
We had two moons;
we unbuttoned our shirts
while we watched the men
ride further and silently away,
past the screen, out to fields
where they dropped their clothes too,
and lay down, and told no one.

Correctional House

We have not learned to close our hands.
They fall to our laps like uniforms,
like letters. Our mother's faces have fragmented,
innocent as Susan Hayward's in *I Want to Live*,
when she sways in black pumps
to the electric chair.

Lucille, the guard
with the Playform tits, smuggles us
lipstick, perms. We say to her, Lucille,
bring us a little Sinatra,
give us the key to the city where we can rest
on the arms of men,
where we can cradle guns of soap
under hot furs. Bring us your crushed corsages,
bring us a steak.

Here, take these hands.
We are tired of touching ourselves.
We are tired of the spring traps of our palms.
Deliver us someplace we can remove these scars
like bracelets from our wrists. Take us
where something is inexplicably wrong,
so that we will feel comfortable: a house
where we can put these hands on a child
who is staring into a face
that has fallen apart,
that will never be ours.

Alias

In sunglasses like dark lakes
I like the way
the car capsules me from conversation,
the smell of the day burning.

I write home, "Wind
through the door is in every house,
land from my window a hard pie."

It was a good house.
Shutters, soup. One day
in the mailbox the face
on the cover was mine, my eyes
in repose, the children unborn.

Clouds collect
in an endless shampoo, the road
before me definite, divine,
shimmering like emulsion. Limousines
carry dark cartons.

In the next town the parade
is always coming, batons
thrashing spoons. Motel
carpets roll out
like tongues.

I take off my many coats.
They hang
themselves. All over
the block are neighbors
calling my new name.

Some Gangster Pain

Eunice is tired of pain, everyone else's.
She wants some gangster pain,
to strut her thick ivories
in a collision of dreams, the pajamas-to-work
dream, the magnolia siege dream.

What ya got there, Eunice, say Johnny and the boys.
Eunice lives behind the bus,
another fleeing place,
riot of exhaust. She doesn't
have much to say,
but she says it, hello.

When the boys talk
she feels her skirt
shift to the corner she took.
She sees them snap their fingers
to no dog. She knows

they wouldn't understand.
She knows her feet point themselves forward
but she keeps walking backwards in rain,
her heels too fast, or the rain seeps
into trees, she can't tell. She likes this street.

Johnny and the boys got on
jackets that twitch.
Eunice wears a lot of accessories. The boys
paint a circle on the wall
the color of lips.

Part III

The Sun Comes Down

The sun comes down to sit in the fruit bowl,
content among oranges.
In mid-epilogue

shadow dramas die on the pavement,
and townspeople lay down
to rest before supper,

some falling peacefully, some snapping awake
before the spiked branches
on the other side of the world.

There is great clarity.
Newspapers lay tossed across yards
like black-foamed batons,

courthouse sprinklers
spin on across the shaved, vitriolic grass,
and the single woman

in the rented room opens the green eyes
of her reputation,
her one good friend

dropping his pants
to the poem engraved
down his thigh.

Harvest

In the grit of threshed maize,
its scent falling across the farm
like the sigh of an old man setting down his tools,
the girl wished for an adult mind.

She wished for action spinning in
on a gunslinger's high black hat,
trouble cast in her footprint.

One day she would think without remorse of childhood,
where she had come to love the colts
with their long, crazy lashes like those of drunken women.
Yesterday, the ring of pitchfork.

The plow's oily skirts made fun of girls
who went to town, but by August
she had seen all the moving pictures.
The teenage beach and the West and the holy East.
She had watched people from the bottom up.

Already she had imagined chariots of bonneted,
rain-faced women, with bullfighters in their suits of light,
riding hell-bent to save her. Each dusk
she took the plow in backwards at full-throttle,
while the farm blurred to a horizon
irresistible as a mirror. Alone in the fields,

she practiced turning
with all the eloquence of the body,
her head leading the way, her hand
held out, cupped, ready for the pair of reins
gods might drop from the dark.

Suddenly the Graves

I would never say anything against the dead.
I would drop my clothes to them
and say yes, see how the sun
won't leave alone
what we cover. My neighborhood
is startingly luminous.
Yesterday yellow tanks steamshovelled
for the underworld. Otters dove
to sleek back their hair.
On the bench a man old as dirt
sat over his death
while teenagers, their hair
bright as planets, chased the greased
and iridescent ducks.

There is no peace in my mind anywhere.
If I nap in this light my grandparents rise
and mix their dominoes, their hands
rinsed of sun but bone-pure.
What if I left with them,
and shed my body? Would I
hear a single, melodious siren
singing the power,
the glory? Or would I
live on, as the earth continues.
With that singing in me.

Johnny Negative and his Ark of Hate

He's drained the world of its color,
its string. The wind
around his finger, all his friends
are capsized strangers, their arms
the waving serpents of his hip, fried crown.

Too many souls rising
in yonder mushroomed air? Burn the brutes,
hark he, let there be
roaches. Torrential rains
in the wrecked ozone, corpses galore,
his surviving baby-loves
got dual animal attraction.

O lost pitchforks of the Black Sea,
rise and pierce the napalm.

O mother of beauty slumming
in beloved red button,
remember the sea,
the beautiful sea.

Insomnia

In some sloppy, ingratiating movement,
wind slips through the weeping hysteria of trees
before winter, boughs in the dark boat

that recurs, but far away,
like the same boat I try
my sleep in. Tonight

there is the embarrassment
of a runaway gown, and the reminder
of the partner beside me,

undone, his breath an odd light.
I have a plot, the morning we wake up
cheerful at the window,

but the plot needs furniture, and these chairs
are really childhood pets barking
their way back, here to take me somewhere,

show me what was
never retrieved. A mob
of wild ideas waits

in the hallway, but there is no
getting up. This is the city
with no moon, and it is useless

turning the day over. In Hong Kong,
the light is leaving
only its suggestion, and soon

it will be mine, bleaching
absolute clarity
hanging over me,

threads begging
connection, the fragments
already disappearing before me.

Tonight I Feel Mortal

Tonight I feel mortal,
like I could never grow another arm
the other two could love.

The important thing is to live winsomely backwards,
unbalm the decisions, good quick ones,
piquant decisions.

You have a theory:
Velcro on hips.
I have a storm glass window,

the possibility for refraction,
just letting the whole thing
refract. Hi,

here is my happy childhood.
I'll do my vigilante pop-up from the shell,
my hands cascading palominos.

You'll read this as a regional voodoo.
The house a vague tug
to cross the street,

I have painted my toenails red.
You have on shiny black shoes.
Our whereabouts are coming.

Premature Reincarnation

After your wordlessness, after loping
from fields that won't hide you,
bitter grass, colors
you lay down in,
for the last time
you will enter.the trees, their music,
and crush leaves to your ear
as when you slept.

Every tree will wink in its complicity.
You'll see the rat
learn to fly
and the owl devoured. You'll run
to pastures your legs burn for,
a sky that can't take you
though you raise your arms.

There will be days of limit,
of indecipherable thought,
but soon your legs will straighten
and your arms tire and hang
so without reluctance
you will walk
into a house, discover
the hideous grass between your teeth,
darkened pads of your hands,
and work day and night
to remove them, to scrub and oil your body
though there is no flight.

You will dream
in a tamed language
you fear others can hear. In the day
in crowds of people or alone
at night in bed the curious will stir

within you, for you
have been struck
from the waters and the fields.
You are not wolf
or snake or hog,
and one day
you must rise without wings.

Goat Without Horns

*an expression once common in New Orleans, and
meaning the Voodoo sacrifice of a young, white child*

Ask, and both black and white
will tell you
no one even their great-grandparents

knew stole a child from its linen,
ran through wooded neighborhoods
and hoarfrost

to Voodoos. No, only cats and chickens
could anyone remember
thrown in the middle air,

no tiny god of the cauldron.
If next morning
the mother was half-awake

at a crib, her hands
searching the caul of absence,
it was a story

everyone made up,
convenient as beasts
preying antebellum maidens,

or the drum-voice
beneath the auction block
at midnight: Yes, what

white folks whispered
to each other
in the dark,

stroking themselves
slowly under bed clothes
while the chandelier

had its way with the moon,
and crosstown
the ash-ringed coals dimmed:

unreadable, untold, child
to fire, sacrificial
burning, child

before man,
the face at the end
of the flare.

The Sky Fills Everything

When the sun was right,
12 noon, and my body
held its shadow,

I counted the trunk's rings,
hay-colored, lion-colored,
to see how many years

I had to live. I wanted both hands
filled with pollen,
black bees at my fingers.

I waited for my heart
to count backwards.
It rose, and a wind

stirred the azalea,
so many wings and no flying.
Today you bring books,

a red-flooded flower. We walk
through the thousand accidents
of nature.

To bring us together
the fractured world
tears and weeps and pulls,

and I trust the body that takes me,
each cell splitting, aching
in memory

of the paradises
where we were
fearless and wild.

In the Willingness of Time to Slow Down

Great heroes are murdered
and children's pets freeze to death,
but we are not there
on those occasions. Instead

I have followed your gestures
to where we must have spent
a mutual childhood, but sometimes
I look in astonishment

at you sleeping
or slicing a lemon,
and am unable to trace what event
led me to you who I suddenly hardly know,

so that again I am a stranger
to the hands
I pull through my hair
in wonder. No one knocks,

no one appears after years of wandering
to say there has been
some horrible mistake,
we must return to the hospital

of your birth that mixed you up, no,
they of the white smoking jackets
and clipboards do not find us
as we pace

from wall to wall,
dazzling the room with talk.
So much talk I have decided
on a single noise

for the hum of content.
In unison, let us low and moan
above the central heat,

and on the ledge

where we never hurled ourselves,
I will reach such a pitch
that the people,
stories below, huddled dot-like

before the public fountain,
will turn away
from spring's first tulip,
alone, and red.

Mad Snow

Slate clapped to a roof,
                    the crows'
dark leather,
          they ache in design,
mad snow—empty themselves
into sense. Somewhere
someone must think they are beautiful.

They make me want your sure mouth. So what if the windows
are sockets,
                    they are lit up
in perfect transparency,
                         avert small talk
to blunt air.

Those hills are fat zones
to point from.
               They let
our bodies slope
                    in loneliness.
My image is out there,
                       on the hill,
burning,
         my scars
like money.

Rush Hour

All day, the important things
leave. Behind the skyline,
the sun is a fast star.
Light seeps
into the city. The street lunges
on its silver belly, turns
back, gives up.
Up steel grids, the city's
last hot breath
pushes itself everywhere
like a stain. They start
to come out, the black suits, men
who can't wait
to loosen their ties. They brandish
briefcases like tense dreams that
just repeat and repeat. Women
exit buildings alone, their hands
shading their eyes, their hands cupped
like hats. Everyone is necessary.
At five o'clock, everyone
wants bourbon, or sleep. Sales
girls lilt past
with a smell of old gardenias, stiletto
heels clicking their song
like castinets. Nylon against flesh,
the swish of skirts. On streetcorners,
newspapers hide faces. Headlines
turn the world
into one small idea. The old drunk
propped on the corner.
is asleep with a smile
on his face that could save
this city. Workers pass
him, think "misplaced brick."

State Line

This blue swell of road
swallows landmarks: tilted silo,
wet cotton fields,
the bucket tied to a well.

For a mile stretch,
nothing much but a man
rushing cows to a barn, cursing
this Texas winter,
the odd snow. The laced slap of wind

spins birds. Caught quick
in a curve, the scream that tears
from the throat, raw
as a black grackle, was one
you might have named.

Bent grace, ribs of wings
raged, your windshield red
as eyes in a field—
you shouldn't have to see this.

Still the sound
stays, humming in the torn window,
the blunt hit of breath, fit of wings
that takes you on your way.

July 5, 1985

Shredded Roman candle,
you have landed here
between tomatoes and Kentucky Wonders
to a July afternoon
in the eighties,
where I am down on my knees
dividing tubers and lifting
the small dead
that fell in the night.

On all fours I am
looking hard into my garden
while the grieved mockingbirds
flit and sing between
hazelnut and telephone pole,
between harmony and terror.

Almost playfully they dip
where you must have dove
after your bright life, after your spectacle
ripened, slanting their wings down
through the lower orbits
of mosquitoes—
those blood angels—closer
and closer to ground, singing,
daring like a tongue
that between the teeth
still manages to praise.

Birthday

I linger
here under banana trees
and the plum that won't bear its fruit.

The imaginary friends
come back, arrange themselves
like instincts. They are tired, they have traveled

through so many rooms,
wondering where did the others go,
who do we love now?

They are such poor witnesses.
Inside the house, where there is champagne,
and sudden, mortal laughter,

my friends are icing a cake.
One licks the knife, another writes
my name in sugar.

You, who have lived
in the trees and the bushes,
there has been no love like yours.

Melon, not cake,
was served, and we sat here,
in the garden,

with the enormous lives of plants.
You were such rightful fauna.
I am not a child.

Who will praise you?
Who will comfort
your infinite loneliness?

I will, says the vagrant rain.
I will, says the orphan crow.

Dead Man's Curve

The screech was heard
by a salesman, new to the area,
who was just then stepping
into the coffee shop
where later he would tell
that riding the last tumultuous angle
a pick-up lost itself
in a hairpin whorl.
He saw it spin
nose to tail, blue smear
before it landed
right side up
and a woman rolled out
saved in the thicket.

For days the woman
would talk of nothing
but how on the other side
of the round and spinning earth
trees froze
in their snowy gowns, animals
huddled beneath ice, but for her
there was suddenly
so much air, then a field
settling like a supple cloth.

No one could get the woman to remember
the green thrill
through resinous pines,
but only the blood rush or spun height
where sky blurs ground,
and the after,
when life turned simple
as a wheel,
and all the gentle ghosts revolved

as clouds stopped
their witless, tumbling motion,

trees bowed, crows lit,
and she looked down
on her grey, receding
town, stacked and vigilant, belonging
to what cannot fall
out of this world
but only deeper in.

People at the counter,
their coffee growing cold,
told and liked to hear
what happened over and over,
and the woman especially
took a liking to the salesman,
even bought everything he had,
and shed a tear when she watched him
drive slowly the same road
out of town, disappearing
around the horizon,
he who had sold all
and did not know
if he would find more towns
on the other side,
or constant night, villages of snow.

The Imaginary Friend

Your name is Desire.
                I got this idea
to give you half my life.
You,
        with the sun-colored bolt of hair,
can live
            in the extravagant room
leaking out my window.
                    White horse, red stair,
and a crow to fly
in the four winds of your walls.

If I become sad,
                I will send
a small bucket
                knocking
down your stairs.
                    But you must come back
with more
            than the drizzle of sand
falling from your hand.

Feast on our life,
                    the steep air
for climbing.
                We can be kin
in an eternal house,
                    your hair falling
to my shoulders
                if my thoughts
become too private.